One Way Ticket From Bali To Hell

A Sister's Story

One Way Ticket From Bali To Hell

A SISTER'S STORY

SUE COOPER - TISDALL

StoryTerrace

Text Jack Cummings, on behalf of StoryTerrace
Design StoryTerrace
Copyright © Sue Cooper – Tisdall
ISBN: 9798773260851

First print November 2021

StoryTerrace

www.StoryTerrace.com

*I dedicate this book to my daughter and son,
Stephanie and Oliver Cooper.*

*Jack Cummings, without whose patience and
understanding this book would have never been written.*

*The numerous people all over the world who it has been
my pleasure and good fortune to meet.*

Many of whom have become close and treasured friends.

*My husband Richard, his sister Christine,
my stepson Sam and stepdaughter Jessica.*

CONTENTS

PROLOGUE   9

1. EARLY YEARS   11

2. CHEF AT WORK   37

3. THE GARDEN LODGE   49

4. MY BROTHER   57

5. THE AFTERMATH   67

6. LOOKING FORWARD   81

PROLOGUE

October 12th 2002 began as a happy Saturday for my family. Things were quiet at Garden Lodge — our family-run guesthouse — so myself, my husband, Ron and our son, Oliver, decided to accompany my daughter, Stephanie, to London for the day, where she was having her weekly singing lesson with Glyn James.

As we walked down Oxford Street to do some shopping, I was suddenly overcome with a profound feeling of anxiety and dread. It hit me out of nowhere, and I was certain that I was having a heart attack. Unbeknownst to me, my father had been hit with the same feelings of anxiety while staying with friends in Spain. Unable to carry on our day trip after my sudden panic attack, Ron, Stephanie, Oliver and I returned home on the train, where the news of a bombing in Bali was announced on TV.

I didn't pay much attention until the newsreader said that the bomb had exploded in Kuta. *That's where my brother was.* I knew instantly that Paul had been killed.

1

EARLY YEARS

My dad, Joseph Hubert John Hussey, was my hero. Before my birth he was stationed in Belgium with the Royal Inniskilling Dragoon Guards, driving tanks during the fragile conclusion of World War Two. On a stroke of luck, he had met my mother, Jean, during his initial training in Yorkshire. As the story goes, Joseph was at the Fox Steelworks Social Club, where he nervously turned down Jean's offer of a dance because he didn't know how to. That didn't matter to Jean, a confident, headstrong young woman who offered to teach him. In those days, Mum worked at the adjoining factory, making umbrella spokes and packed parachutes during the war. She was a caring young woman and used all her wages to support her mother – who'd been widowed twice – as well as her older brother, Ernest. He shared her confidence and work ethic and later became a squadron leader in the RAF, earning many commendations.

Joe and Jean quickly fell in love, but because Dad was

soon to be posted abroad, their engagement was quite unorthodox. Dad proposed in a letter and had to give Mum £25 to buy her own ring. They married during his brief leave on 3rd September 1945, and I've always admired my mother, knowing that she had to organise the whole thing.

The years leading up to my birth weren't easy for my parents. Dad left the army without his formal discharge papers, returning to his trade as a bricklayer. They lived in a prefab on Hollands Avenue in Folkestone, before moving to Swindon, Wiltshire, after my dad joined the RSPCA. Before my birth, Mum tragically lost two babies – painful events which she never spoke about. One day my dad came home to find her playing with a puppy. Not one to mince his words, he said, "Isn't it time we had a real baby to play with?"

***

I arrived on 23rd July 1952. Most of my earliest memories are tied to my dad, who was a real animal lover. He bred golden retrievers and showed cocker spaniels, winning the Rose Bowl Award with his prized spaniel, Dandy. He built an aviary in the garden and kept budgies who dazzled Paul and I with their wonderful array of colours. Dad wasn't just passionate about animals, he was industrious too, once swapping a golden retriever puppy for a new TV with the local chemist. Alongside this ingenious nature, he was a caring man and doted on myself and Paul. I have never forgotten how he quit his smoking habit and used the money to buy us a custard slice from Elizabeth's bakery every Saturday. I couldn't have loved him more.

Dad's love of animals went beyond the pets we kept. He was inspired to join the RSPCA after witnessing the poor treatment of animals at Maidstone Zoo. The collection of exotic animals was owned by an ageing Sir Garrard, and rising costs and new standards of welfare meant the zoo's conditions had become sub-par. I imagine the poor living situation of the elephants and chimpanzees struck a chord with my dad, who was never one to back down from a sense of duty.

Within a year or so of joining the RSPCA, Dad was a respected inspector, winning a special commendation for his animal rescue efforts in the Canvey Island floods. He was promoted to Senior Inspector in 1957, and shortly thereafter we relocated to Bodmin, Cornwall, at the RSPCA's request. I embraced anything that meant being close to my dad, and in time I became his trusty sidekick. When I wasn't at school, he'd let me jump in the van and tag along to the livestock markets he diligently inspected. If ever there was an oil spill, he would bring home all manner of tarred seabirds for me to carefully scrub clean under the outside tap. From time to time, I'd accompany him to disused tin mine shafts, watching from a safe distance as he risked his life to coax out the heifers who had cluelessly wandered in.

Despite the fact I was a real daddy's girl, I was also an independent and adventurous youngster. From the age of six, I'd spend my long summers up in Yorkshire, staying in Deepcar with Granny Shaw. I always loved visiting her because she afforded me special privileges – like letting me have my toys in bed. If I wasn't with Granny Shaw, I'd stay with Uncle Willis and Aunty Violet, who were kind to me and always made sure I had a friend to spend time with. Those long afternoons were spent adventuring in the hills with my lifelong friend Elizabeth Day. Our wonderful connection ran through the generations; Elizabeth's dad was godfather to Paul and had been Mum's best friend at school.

Meanwhile, Mum and Dad became real community pillars in Bodmin. Together they ran the town's football club, organising garden parties, dances and events to help bring the club out of debt. Of course they had to be smart, and Dad would always make sure I had the winning ticket for the giant white teddy bear, just so he could use it again at the next raffle. I also recall waiting for hours to cheer on Dr Barbara Moore as she passed through Bodmin on her walk from John O'Groats to Land's End.

Eventually however we left Bodmin and moved to Lyminge. Dad had resigned from the RSPCA to return to his trade as a bricklayer. He'd become increasingly upset at having to put down perfectly healthy dogs just because people didn't want them. Of course, Dad needed an ambitious project to keep him occupied, and he set about building a bungalow in Lyminge with £5 in his pocket. My prized jobs were mixing endless buckets of plaster and coating every inch of woodwork with dreaded grey primer. I wasn't one to complain, but the monotony drove me mad.

That said, it certainly taught me the value of hard work. By the time I started at St Leonard's Secondary School for Girls, I would work odd jobs whenever the opportunity arose. Every Saturday and Sunday I'd visit Mrs. Horton at Shilston House over the road, where she'd pay me tuppence-per-tray for cleaning the muck and straw from freshly laid eggs. On other occasions, she'd have me creosoting the chicken coops, and later in the spring I'd work alongside her handyman, Dart, picking asparagus during the precious six-week harvesting window. To this day, fresh asparagus served with warm butter always takes me back to Mrs Horton's garden. Of course, this hard work didn't bother me – I had inherited my dad's work ethic.

My great passion at this time was ballroom dancing, and I attended weekly lessons at the Margaret Ratcliffe School of Ballroom Dancing. There I became skilled in ballroom and Latin American dance, partnering with a girl called Sally from Dymchurch. On weekends, we'd venture to the beach together. Sally later moved to Spain where she made her career as a hairdresser, but we continued to write to one another and are still in touch to this day.

When I was at home, Paul and I would devise our own

entertainment. Together we'd build camps or grass circus rings, entertaining the neighbours with shows featuring our golden retriever. It was a happy childhood, and my life in Lyminge meant the world to me.

Mum was similarly minded and put family values above all else. She worked at Bobbies Snack Bar in Folkestone during the day and spent her evenings cleaning offices. She was an expert at making a little go a long way, and I've never forgotten the smell of her delicious stews and fantastic cakes wafting through the house.

During her time cleaning offices, Mum met Margaret and Ron Cooper, a couple who were also building a bungalow and living in a caravan on-site. Mum said they could come over and take a bath whenever they needed to. I've always wondered if the offer was out of generosity or because of the smell! Regardless, they soon became firm family friends. Ron helped Dad to wallpaper my room, and the four of them even went to Spain together, which was my parents' first holiday abroad.

Eventually my Dad was offered a job on a fruit farm in Bekesbourne as a maintenance manager, where we were to live on-site in one of the purpose-built bungalows. It was a good offer, but I was distraught. I didn't want to move schools, leave my friends or stop my dancing classes. Despite only being 12, I had worked hard to create a happy little life for myself in Lyminge. In Bekesbourne I found myself on a farm in the middle of nowhere, riding my bike for miles in all weathers just to catch the bus to an unfamiliar school – which I hated.

It was during our time on the farm that I also discovered my frailty at the sight of human blood. Paul came home one day with a great gash across his lip. He'd come off his bike after skidding in the gravel and was losing a lot of blood. Mum left me to look after Paul; she wanted to go find Dad to take him to hospital. When they returned however, Paul was the one looking after me. I had passed out in the hallway, knocking over several potted plants in the process. I can skin rabbits and gut fish with ease, but I always pass out at the sight of human blood.

Despite these challenges, I performed better at Sturry Secondary School than I had at St Leonard's School For Girls. I was very surprised to receive the form progress prize on Speech Day – a cookery book which is still in regular use!

Meanwhile, at home I was once again faced with the dreaded primer and plaster. Dad was never happy living in someone else's property and eventually talked his boss into selling him a piece of land in the nearby village of Littlebourne. Despite the chore of having to assist him once more, I was grateful that I no longer had to ride my bike to catch the bus to school. These projects continued when my grandad came to live with us soon afterwards. More space was required, so Dad built another beautiful detached bungalow overlooking the river. During that project, Dad taught me how to lay bricks.

Moving to the village brought many happy memories and special friendships. A Belgian boy named Jean-Marie whose father supplied fruit trees to the farm came to stay with us. Mum was happy to host Jean-Marie and immediately christened him 'John'. She couldn't understand why a boy was called Jean and certainly wasn't going to have two people called Jean in the house!

The name stuck and a lifelong friendship followed. Over the years, we regularly visited John in Belgium. During one visit he drove us to Opoeteren, where my dad had been stationed. The local lady in the post office immediately recognised him and threw an impromptu party in the evening which the whole village attended. It amazed me to see how loved and respected my dad was in this small community so far from home.

Mum and Dad later attended John and Monique's wedding in Belgium, and their eldest son was a pageboy at my first wedding. Years later, John and Monique came to stay and support me following Dad's passing, and during their most recent visit in 2018 we celebrated 50 years of friendship.

Mum was always happy to have foreign students stay with us. Olivia – a girl from Germany – became like a sister to me. I later visited her in Frankfurt, and her father took us to the opera in Wiesbaden. It was exquisite but boring – and something we still laugh about to this day. I'll never forget the sight of all the performers prancing around with sheep's heads on.

These early experiences inspired the way I ran the Garden Lodge guesthouse many years later. Like Mum, I had many students stay with me, and I greatly value the wonderful connections I have made all over the world.

***

By this point, I was earning money whenever I had the opportunity. On Saturdays I would work at Ricemans department store in Canterbury for eight shillings and sixpence a day – equivalent to about 40p today! Needless to say that most of it went on the bus fare, so I also took a job at the corn stores in Littlebourne. On Tuesdays every week I'd babysit for Sandra and Gillian Coates-Smith, but I was never allowed to accept any payment for this as their parents were friends of Mum and Dad.

My parents' sense of hospitality continued during our time in the village. Lutgart (the niece of Helen from the post office in Opoeteren) came to stay one summer and we became great friends. Together we went strawberry picking and got very sunburnt. As a pale redhead, Lutgart's back became one huge blister, which was so painful she had to walk around the bed rather than roll over, just to reposition herself!

Between my various jobs, childhood adventures and everything I had learned from Mum and Dad, I developed into a headstrong teenager. Above all else, I hated people doubting me or telling me I couldn't do something. When my food and nutrition teacher told me I wasn't good enough to take the subject at O-level, it made my blood boil. I proceeded to get the highest pass mark in the class just to teach her a lesson. It was through this that I discovered my aptitude for cooking, but it was proving Miss White wrong that was the sweetest victory.

A very proud daughter looks on as her father is presented with medals and commendations

Dad with his beloved golden retrievers when they lived in Holland's Avenue in Folkestone

Dad, Susan, Paul and Snowy in back garden at Bodmin

Granny Shaw in fancy dress

Granny Shaw, Auntie Underhill, Mum and Susan waiting for the Queen to pass in Swindon

Joe, my dad, with his great gran, brother Jack and sister Joyce

Ivy Hussey, my gran

My Grandad, Joseph Wellman Hussey

Mum when she was crowned May Queen

Mum & Dad on their wedding day, 3rd September 1945

Mum on her wedding day with brother Ernest and her mother

Susan 15 weeks old with proud Mum

Susan 7 and a half months with Dandy, the prize-winning cocker spaniel

Susan with Dad & David Brooms Horse, 1954

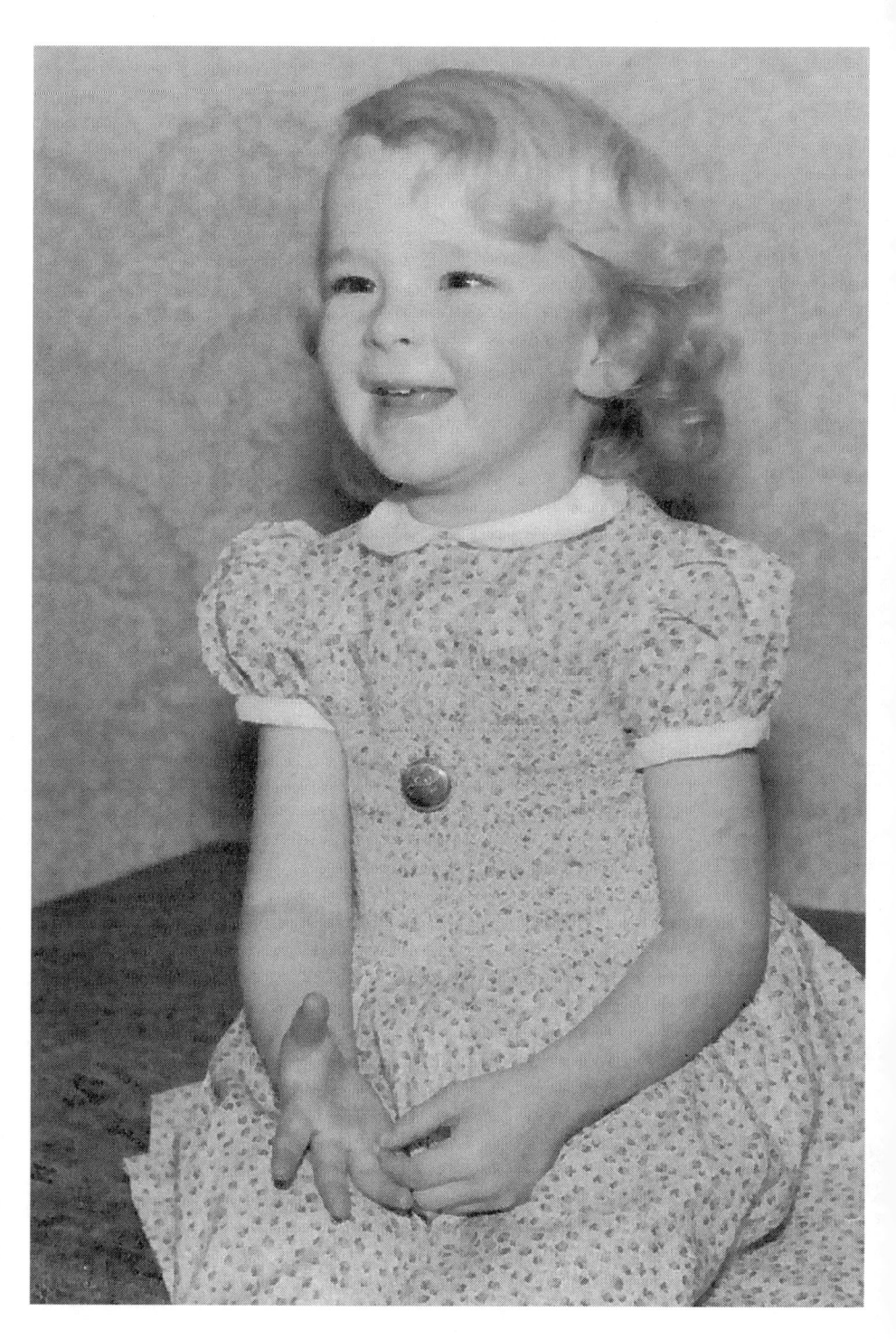

Susan, 4th December 1954. 2 years old

Susan, Mum and Paul

The day I left school, 22nd July 1970

This is my mum, Jean Walker with all her relatives - the Mates

2

CHEF AT WORK

I started on the General Catering course at Thanet Catering College when I was 18 years old. I've never forgotten my very first lesson – not because of any culinary achievements, but because our teacher cut the end of his finger off whilst demonstrating the 'correct' way to chop an onion. Needless to say, we never let him forget it, and when I bumped into Mr Stiefelhagen a few years ago, I couldn't resist asking, "How's the finger?" Although I enjoyed my catering classes, student life wasn't particularly exciting. The campus was 20 miles away from my family home in Littlebourne, so I spent Monday to Friday in digs at Ramsgate and the weekends at home earning money. In those days we didn't get generous maintenance loans, so my evenings were spent doing my homework, eating supper and not much else. That said, my roommate Susan Llewellyn and I occasionally treated ourselves to a night out at Nero's, the local club.

Meanwhile, I quickly began to find my calling as a chef-in-training. I loved savoury cooking and took pride in making delicate soups and sauces. Mum, Dad and Paul became my practising taste-testers and spent weeks sampling my beer and onion soup for a competition sponsored by Shepherd Neame, the local brewery whose beer entrants were expected to utilise. Later I entered the 'Decorated Cold-Sweet for Eight' category at the prestigious Salon Culinaire and was awarded the Silver Diploma – something I am still immensely proud of.

Aside from honing my cooking skills, weekends at home were no different from my early teens, and I was always working to help fund my studies. On Saturdays I'd work at the mushroom farm and my Sundays were spent alongside Mum and Susan, waitressing at the Old Tudor Tea Rooms in Wickhambreaux. Meanwhile, everyone on our course became very close. There is something about the catering profession that really brings people together – even for trainees at college. I remember meeting a lad called Julian Paton-Smith en-route to class on my very first day, and I am still friends with him and his brother, Stephen, now. Whilst the students all had their strengths and weaknesses, class CA1D always stuck up for one another and helped each other out. Often, we'd go en masse to one another's houses for the evening. Our mums were always eager to feed us up – we might've been chefs, but they still thought of us as starving students!

My own training went from strength-to-strength during those three years at Thanet Catering College. Aside from cooking, I was a very good waitress, and the principal would always have me wait on his table when guests attended the college. These skills were put to the ultimate test In 1977 when our whole class was asked to wait at the Queen's Silver Wedding lunch at the Guildhall in London. I was immensely proud of the experience and made sure to tell all my family and friends. I loved the fact that even as students we were trusted to help out at prestigious events, and we later managed the exhibitors' tents at Farnborough Air Show. This was a grand experience made all the better by the fantastic tips we picked up on the bigger tables.

Paul meanwhile was very studious as a teenager, and Dad always thought he would become an architect. He excelled at woodwork and built his own drawing board from scratch, but to everyone's surprise he followed in my footsteps and decided to attend catering college. I am not sure why Paul decided to do this – perhaps he saw how happy I was training to be a chef. That said, he wasn't interested in the hard work of being in the kitchen. He opted to go into hotel management, and would go on to become one of the top managers in the world. My brother could turn his hand to anything, and it saddens me to think what else Paul might've achieved if he wasn't taken from us.

***

I must admit that my first year or two as a professional chef is hard to piece together. I moved between several jobs, and although I was never out of work, I didn't feel settled. My first position as a so-called chef was at the White Horse Pub in Chilham, where I was put behind the bar carving joints of meat. This was a waste of my training, and to make matters worse I was a terrible carver. What upset me most however was the fact that the wing-mirror of my beloved Mini was smashed off while parked in the village square during my shift. That sealed the deal, and I left the job after a week. I might've been new, but I certainly had my standards.

Shortly afterwards I moved to the Rabb Inn in Dover, where I stayed in staff accommodation in the inn. Mum came with me to help me move in and wasn't happy with the state of the place, proclaiming that her daughter wasn't used to living in a slum – much to the surprise of the manager!

Mum was a lot like me. She always spoke her mind and the owners must've paid attention because I was promptly moved to better living quarters. Yet again however the work was beneath my training, and I spent long hours deep-frying fish – most of which I ended up losing under the fryer basket. As you might expect, I didn't stay at the Rabb Inn for very long either. My reasoning this time however was that I started suffering from bouts of dizziness and vertigo, which led to a diagnosis of Meniere's disease. This lifelong condition has caused several bouts of BPPV (vertigo), although thankfully these are fairly infrequent and can be kept under control with special manoeuvres.

My career took a different turn when I received a surprising phone call from Mr Preston – the principal of Thanet Catering College. He drove me and one of my old tutors, Pat Frape, to Luton Hoo, where I was interviewed by Lady Zia Wernher for the role of her personal chef. I wasn't happy with the salary I was offered, but the Countess immediately agreed to my request for more money! As it happens, her best friend was Lady Susan Hussey – then a lady-in-waiting to the Queen – and I think the fact we shared a name went in my favour!

At Luton Hoo I lived in the mansion house in beautiful accommodation. It was a stark contrast to my time at the Rabb Inn, but I disliked the work. By that point, the Countess was in her 80s, stuck in her ways and accustomed to a long life of people waiting on her hand-and-foot. She was incredibly fussy and refused to eat *anything* that had even looked at an onion. Each morning she'd demand to inspect the menu, and as you can well imagine I thought she was a real bitch.

I left Luton Hoo shortly after the Countess had a screaming fit over some burnt Yorkshire puddings, thinking I'd ruined her precious silverware. Over the next couple of years, I turned my hand to various jobs. I was part of an all-girls team at the George and Dragon in Fordwich and worked as the catering manager at the head post office in Maidstone. During my time there I lived in Bearsted with a lovely couple called Val and Peter Sime, as well as their two young daughters. I also took work on and off as a relief school dinner lady, but spent most of the time getting lost because I never knew which school I was supposed to be at!

Thankfully, by this point I was working at the White Horse in Boughton part-time in the evenings (not to be confused with the White Horse in Chilham!). These were long days, and I'd work as a dinner lady at Sir Roger Manwood's School from 7.00am until 3.30pm, before heading to the White Horse from 6.00pm until closing time for some real cooking. Fortunately, the White Horse was a job which I really enjoyed, and I was grateful when John and Yvonne Durcan (the owners) asked me to run the kitchen full-time. This was a decision made easier by the fact that I'd left my position as a relief school dinner lady after requiring a third operation for spurs on my heels – which required a lengthy hospital stay.

After moving between so many jobs and often feeling unsettled and under-utilised, joining the White Horse was when I really found my rhythm as a chef. I would turn out 200 bar snacks every day, as well as cooking for a full restaurant and private function room. I loved that John and Yvonne trusted my judgement and gave me the freedom to cook what I liked. Working at the White Horse was like being part of one big, happy family. There was Ricardo, our Spanish waiter, and John was a funny and easy-going boss. Yvonne meanwhile has remained one of my closest friends over the years – she was a great support to me when I had my stroke and remains a true and valued friend.

I made the mistake of briefly leaving the White Horse when I was head-hunted by Kim and Pamela Pardoe to run the kitchen of their new restaurant in Folkestone – The Pullman. I knew this was a fantastic opportunity which I couldn't pass on, but was swayed by the fact it meant being closer to my parents. My memories of working there are tarnished by one experience which really infuriated me. The restaurant received a glowing feature review in *The Caterer* magazine, with shining praise for all of The Pullman's signature dishes. The problem was that there was no mention of my name – the food was all credited to Kim and Pam. This struck me as deeply unfair because I was the one who created the dishes and designed the menu. To make matters worse, when I confronted them they simply shrugged and said, "It's our restaurant, and that's how it is." They had no desire to have the article amended or ensure that I was credited. I was furious. Those dishes were my creations, and I hated being so blatantly overlooked. You don't work as hard as I do to be ignored like that.

Thankfully I moved back to the White Horse shortly afterwards and quickly settled back into running the kitchen. The wonderful thing about being so connected to the pub was that in many ways it felt like I never left. John and Yvonne welcomed me back with open arms, which is something I was incredibly grateful for.

That said, I knew they were appreciative of me in ways that Kim and Pam weren't and knew they would have struggled to find such a hard-working, dedicated chef. Needless to say, working at the White Horse brought with it many cherished memories. I can vividly picture Tarek Sharif (son of the legendary thespian Omar Sharif), who stayed there whilst studying at university. He loved my treacle tarts, scotch eggs and quiches and would stay up until the early hours playing backgammon with John. God knows how much small change they gambled over the years, and each morning I'd quip, "So who owns the pub today?"

Tarek Sharif wasn't the only famous name to come through the pub. A young student by the name of Gary Rhodes was my washer-up and went on to become a celebrity chef famed for his modern take on classic British food, until his untimely death in 2019.

Of course, despite being a hard-working, switched-on chef, I was certainly forgetful in other ways. More often than not I'd leave my car lights on while at work, and the mechanics next door at Motorway Sports Cars became accustomed to having to charge up my car battery in return for platefuls of chips for their lunch. John gave me a lot of stick when he found out that he was paying in potatoes to compensate for my forgetfulness!

As you might expect, I was always in charge in the kitchen and could dial up the volume if need be. My friend Joyce was my regular washer-up and once attempted to make a batch of mayonnaise which promptly curdled. Of course, I went mad because of the 50 or so eggs she'd used, and a shouting match ensued. Eventually, one of the bar staff popped their head into the kitchen and joked that I needed to speak up because the restaurant up the road couldn't hear exactly how many eggs were used.

There are of course countless other anecdotes from my happy years at the White Horse, but the sentiment is much the same: I loved going to work, I loved working hard and I loved the laughter. Naturally, I didn't have time for many serious relationships. I once went on a date with one of the regulars by the name of Alistair Crawford. He would ask me to have a drink with him when I finished work every evening. To my surprise, when I finally agreed he told me to bring my passport, and we flew to the racecourse at Ostend, Belgium, for the day. It turned out that he was a high-flying racehorse owner, and we had so much champagne on the plane that I don't recall much about the day itself.

My friend Alison and I used to spend every Saturday at Canterbury Rugby Club, either serving drinks from behind the bar or chatting to the lovely men in the Decadents Corner! We were both made vice presidents of the club. Later, I was briefly engaged to a local rugby lad, but promptly threw the ring back in his face when I found out he was seeing someone else.

Things changed when I started growing closer to Ron – the same Ron who had babysat me when I was younger and had become a close family friend. By this point, his wife Margaret had died, and I got into the habit of popping in for a cup of tea on the way home from work. Initially this was because I felt sorry for him – he always seemed like a lonely, lost soul. Eventually however he told my Dad that he was growing fond of me, and although this was a big surprise to my parents, I already had an inkling, because Ron had bought me a new car – he was fed up with my Mini breaking down!

From this point on, things moved forward quickly between myself and Ron. Despite this, I was terrified when he invited me to visit his family in Banbury, Oxfordshire. Thankfully, I was relieved when I realised that I knew most of them anyway. I've never forgotten how excited his dad was as we stepped through the door and proudly proclaimed, "Ron's got a girlfriend!" This was news to me, but I didn't contest. In truth I'd grown to love Ron, and I still miss him dearly.

ONE WAY TICKET FROM BALI TO HELL

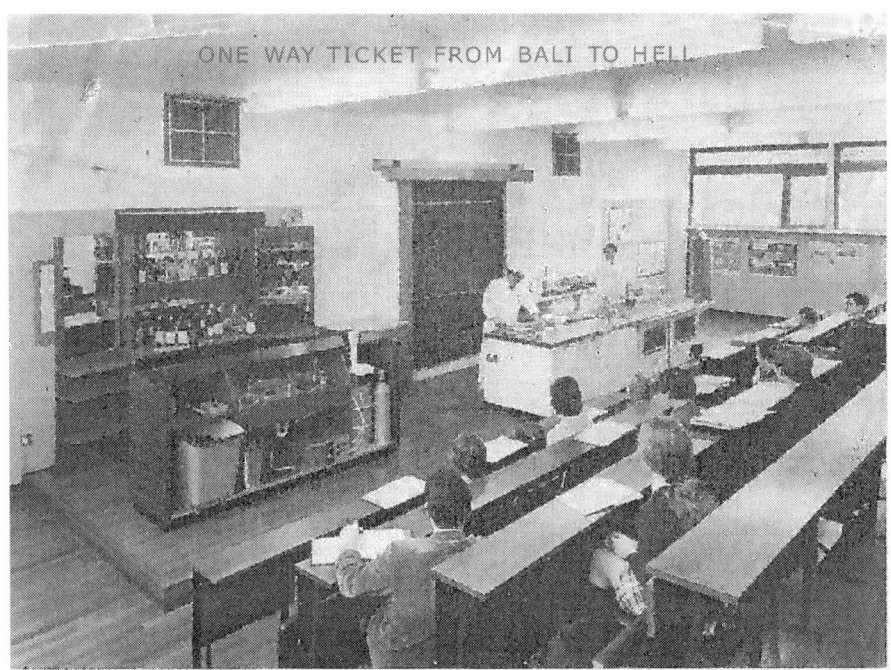

View of the Lecture Demonstration Theatre

Practical Training in the Pastry Kitchen

Pastry kitchen and demonstration kitchen at catering college

Garden Lodge

3

THE GARDEN LODGE

By the time Ron and I married in 1984, I had moved on from the White Horse. John had made me redundant a couple of years prior in the hope that he could replace me with a cheap catering student. Of course, I wasn't going to be stepped on like that and took him to an employment tribunal – which I won. Despite this, I couldn't hold a grudge against John, and he was waiting for me outside the court to suggest we go for a drink and make amends. Despite the fact I won the case, we quickly put everything behind us.

Although John offered me my job back, I'd already been offered a better-paid position at the Granville pub in Lower Hardres – something I took great pleasure in informing him about. Later, by the time Ron and I married, I was working at John Parker & Sons Steelworks as director's chef in the boardroom, and I soon became pregnant with our first child. We had to get a move on because Ron was 50 and I was 32 – we knew we had no time to spare in starting a family. Stephanie arrived on 5th October 1984 and Oliver was born 51 weeks later on 28th September 1985. It never ceases to amaze me that for one week each year they are the same age!

I loved being a mum, but both births were challenging for me. I had low estriols which meant that my placenta wasn't feeding the baby properly. The 10 weeks leading up to Stephanie's birth were spent bedridden in hospital, and I inevitably returned with the same problem the following year whilst pregnant with Oliver. Of course the nurses all found this hilarious, announcing to the ward, "She's back again!"

Keeping in line with my busy lifestyle, we moved into our new home the day after Oliver was born. Thankfully they were both wonderful babies and slept well from a young age, which was helpful given the fact that there was so much to sort out. We spent most of that first month living in one room out of plastic bags whilst we got the heating sorted. Despite this, I still made sure that Stephanie had a first birthday party amongst all the tea chests in the old dining room.

Although I kept working at John Parker & Sons, by this point I was tired of making money for other people and had set my heart on converting our house into a B&B. It was right on the main road between Folkestone and Canterbury so I knew it was in a prime position. We set about organising the rooms and preparing for business, and Ron placed a sign out front officially declaring the Garden Lodge open for guests. Of course, we quickly decided to bring the sign back inside because we weren't quite ready to open, but in the meantime our very first guest had arrived. She knocked on the door and, upon noticing my golden retriever, declared that she didn't like dogs and preferred cats. Despite the fact that this was my first guest, I wasn't taking any nonsense when it came to our golden retriever, who'd been lovingly bred by my dad. "Well that's fine," I said, "I don't like cats, and I'm not getting rid of my dog for anyone."

Business picked up quickly, and Ron came home from work to find our lounge full of guests – neither of us could get in there! So we quickly set about building an extension, and in the meantime had converted the big open loft into individual bedrooms. Much like my dad's projects when I was a child, this was a big family effort. I remember the plumber turned out to be a relative of my dad's, and they spent so long nattering about the old times that I had to remind them that we had a job to do!

When we weren't busy with guests, we always hosted students at the Garden Lodge, and many stayed with us over the years. They usually came from abroad in order to learn English, and several stayed for more than a year. Our first foreign guests were six Italian students, and we became very close to one girl in particular called Patrizia. We later visited her at Lake Como, and Stephanie even went to stay with her when she was six years old. She shared the same adventurous spirit that I'd had all those years earlier during my long childhood summers up north, and we were amazed when Stephanie came home a month later speaking fluent Italian.

I've lost track of the number of wonderful students I have hosted over the years. There was Delphine – whose entire family must've stayed with me at some point over the years! – as well as Liesel, who fell in love with our golden retriever the moment she stepped through the door. Then there was Christina, a Swiss girl who came here for the riding school at Limes Farm. After staying with us the night before, she disliked the state of the school's accommodation and opted to stay with us over the next two years. I helped her get her papers to remain in this country, and she now owns her own riding school in Royal Wootton Bassett.

There was also Atsuko from Japan who was learning to ride horses, and she was in such a state of nerves before she took her road safety test that I felt like I was taking it! Thankfully, she passed.

Of course, who could forget Arnaud, who came to stay with me in order to learn the transport business through a company called Intercity Trucks. Over the next year, Arnaud became like a member of the family. When his time learning the trade came to an end, I got him a job at Sainsbury's, and I've never forgotten his first day on the checkouts when he held up a mysterious vegetable and asked me what it was called.

"That's an onion!" I responded.

We later attended Arnaud's wedding in France, and he requested that Stephanie perform at the reception. My daughter is an incredibly talented singer. We didn't know she had it in her until she performed 'Wind Beneath My Wings' for a competition at Studio 6, bringing all of us to tears. Stephanie really thrived growing up in the B&B environment. She was social and enjoyed being among the guests, and is incredibly talented at performing arts. I loved watching her dance. She attended Studio 6 for dancing lessons five times a week. Later, Stephanie was asked by one of our guests at the Garden Lodge to perform as the support artiste to The Drifters at a charity event in Derby.

Oliver was quiet and preferred being at home with the family. I remember having to pay him just so he would go to Beavers. Despite this, he is incredibly kind and caring. I remember he once came home from school having been asked what his favourite book was. I asked him what he said, and his reply was, "Well I told them that I'd never read a book!" The irony is that Oliver came to love writing and has gone on to become an author.

***

Although we started as a B&B, we grew over the years into a successful guesthouse. We ran a 32-seater restaurant which was open to the public and eventually installed a heated swimming pool, luxury hot tub and sauna. My ambition was to open up a spa but sadly this dream was cut short when I had my stroke in 2010.

As soon as the bungalow next door went up for sale, Dad sold the home he had shared with my mum and snapped it up. Dad always wanted to be close to the action and knocked a hole through the wall so he could come straight into the Garden Lodge without ever having to take his slippers off. It was amazing to watch my dad flourish, and he relished every opportunity to help out. He pressed all of the bed linen for our bedrooms and would hang dozens of bed sheets on multiple lines across his garden, often joking that he was running his own Chinese laundry. I remember once that an inspector complained about a crease in the bed sheets. I dared her to go voice her grievance to my 80-year-old dad next door, and that soon shut her up!

Aside from the students who stayed with us over the years, we had many long-term guests from all walks of life, and we saw our fair share of love and heartache! There was Bill, who was staying with his girlfriend at the time when they abruptly fell out. She asked him to leave, but he said he liked it here and wasn't going anywhere. Bill ended up staying with us for years until he moved to work in Thailand. I was both surprised and happy when he asked me to be his witness at his wedding in Phuket.

Other friendships have really proven their worth since Paul was murdered. I remember John and Betty Radstake from Melbourne, Australia, knocking on our door late one night in desperate need of accommodation. They returned the favour years later during a visit to Melbourne when everything was fully booked up because of the Melbourne Cup. Betty insisted we stay at their home, and we've always laughed about how my hospitality came full circle!

Perhaps my closest friend who I met through the Garden Lodge is Sue Johnson, who appeared on my doorstep when we first opened with an offer to help get my paperwork in order. Her husband had just left her, and I think she was in need of the company. 32 years later, she has become my most trusted friend and is still trying to get me straight!

Then there were the countless impromptu barbecues we hosted over the years, and I will always cherish the memories of those wonderful summer evenings spent with good friends like Terry & Val, Mick & Eileen and many, many others.

I am immensely proud of all that we achieved at the Garden Lodge. One year we were runner-up for the best B&B in South East England, and our motto greeted every guest as they walked through the door: *Arrive as strangers, leave as friends.* I never realised just how grateful I would be for those friendships until Paul was murdered. In many ways, I wish that the rest of my story could be a simple, happy continuation of my life as a mother and guesthouse owner, but the reality is far more painful.

Paul with Michael Crawford at The Hotel Como in Melbourne

4

MY BROTHER

This brings us back to that fateful day in London on October 12th 2002. I'll never forget the moment that I burst into tears whilst walking down Oxford Street. Overwhelmed by anxiety and dread, I returned home to find the news of a bombing in Bali being announced on TV. When I heard that the explosion had occurred in Kuta, I knew instantly that Paul had been killed.

As I mentioned at the very start of my story, Dad was struck by the same feelings whilst staying with friends in Spain. He turned to them at the exact moment my brother was murdered, his face ashen and his eyes filled with tears.

"What's wrong, Joe?" they asked.

"Something's happened to my Paul... he's dead."

In truth, Dad always knew when something was wrong with myself or Paul. I suffered from terrible sea sickness whenever I crossed the English Channel, and Dad would share my nausea despite being safe on dry land. As far as I can recall, this sixth sense was something which had been passed down through the generations on his mother's side. Dad used to recall a story of the night his mother laid an extra place at the dinner table when he was serving in the Army. Naturally, his father asked what the extra place was for.

"That's for our Joe," she'd reply, "he's hurt and he's coming home."

As it happened she was right. It was the very evening Dad had broken his leg. My dad inherited her gift, and although it's hard to understand the origins of this sixth sense, it speaks volumes of the love between our family.

***

When I saw that the bomb had exploded in Kuta, I immediately dialled Paul's phone number. There was no answer, so my next call was to the Saphir Hotel, one of the two establishments in Bali where he served as general manager.

If there was any hope in my mind that Paul was unharmed, this faded when he failed to answer my call. My brother always picked up the phone to me. Every morning the first thing I'd do before breakfast service was turn on the computer and talk to Paul. He was incredibly supportive and helpful to me while I was running the Garden Lodge, even though he was on the other side of the world. He designed the logo and the menus and was my go-to support whenever I was struggling with anything technical.

Paul's duty manager, Mr Syardi, immediately picked up my call to the Saphir, but he didn't share my urgency. "Mr Paul has finished his shift," he said. "But don't worry, the explosion was four miles away from here – I'm sure he is fine."

By this point, I knew that I had to trust my instinct and ordered him to go and check Paul's room. When the duty manager found it to be locked, I demanded he break the door down. Of course he was reluctant, but I knew it was a matter of emergency.

"I will take full responsibility for the bloody door!" I cried. "Break it down!"

They didn't need telling twice, and when they discovered that Paul wasn't in his room, they too realised that something bad had happened. It must be said that I am grateful that Paul's staff trusted my instinct during those frantic first few minutes following the news of the blast. I had met many of them during a visit to Bali earlier in the year when Ron had won a holiday to Thailand through his performance at work. I wasn't going to South-East Asia without seizing the opportunity to see my brother and spun the airline a sad story about how I hadn't seen my brother in years. Thankfully they allowed us to divert to Bali for two weeks. This would be the first of 14 trips to Indonesia over the next two decades – and the only one which took place under happy circumstances.

Whilst Paul's trusted management team began rallying staff to search for him, I immediately called the Foreign Office to find out more information about what was going on, what they were doing and how they could help me. I'll never forget the anger and disbelief I felt when my calls were met with endless automated messages and hold lines. I'll never forget how the insensitivity of their inept protocols made me feel. I'll never forget how it began 20 years of misery at the ongoing mishandling of the tragedy by the Foreign Office.

Eventually I thought, *Screw the Foreign Office*, and decided to focus on my contacts in Bali to help locate Paul. By this point his staff –as well as many guests – had begun rallying together in an effort to begin searching for my brother. Over the next two days, a remarkable 300 people joined the cause, and I thank each one of those loyal staff and kind-hearted holidaymakers from the bottom of my heart. Their efforts to find my brother even drew international recognition, and months later my dad was brought to tears by a beautiful letter from Gerald Moors, a member of the Canadian Coastguard group who were staying at the hotel. He praised the selfless search for Paul and wrote about how beloved my brother must've been.

In truth, this was a feeling expressed by all who knew and worked with Paul during his illustrious career in hotel management. As you will recall, he followed in my footsteps and attended Thanet Catering College, beginning his career working as a chef in a variety of restaurants. Notably, he spent time as a member of the Royal Household as a footman at Buckingham Palace and later joined the University of Kent at Canterbury as a senior chef.

The parallels between our early careers speaks volumes about the similarities between us, but inevitably Paul was destined for the hotel industry. He joined the Hotel de la Plage in Jersey as assistant manager, before heading to the Sheraton Skyline at Heathrow, where he oversaw record success. It therefore came as no surprise when he was asked to lead the newly-opened Sheraton in Edinburgh, underscoring my brother's portfolio of UK experience.

Paul's greatest triumphs however came when he relocated to Australia in 1989, in order to manage the prestigious Hotel Como in Melbourne. This was a real step-up and took my brother to the world stage of hotel management. Of course he excelled at the challenge, guiding Hotel Como to the rank of 5-star superior deluxe – the first of its kind in Australia.

I still remember my heartache on the day that Paul left for Melbourne, yet I was immensely proud of all that he was set to achieve. My brother was a private and humble man, but he elevated the Como to public renown, where it quickly became the must-stay place for all manner of celebrities. Michael Crawford, Tom Jones and Neil Diamond were among the many stars to pass through its doors. Paul used to drink with Billy Connolly and even played host to Dannii Minogue's hen night. On one of my parents' many trips to Australia to visit Paul, Mum excitedly told me that they'd been joined by Dame Edna Everage for breakfast at Hotel Como every morning! I always used to think how lucky my brother was to have met so many celebrities, but in truth they were lucky to have met him. I'd give anything to spend another moment with Paul.

Although we missed him dearly, Australia became a second home for Paul, and he was awarded dual-citizenship in 1996 – the same year that the Hotel Como was granted its 5-star superior deluxe rating. Of course, Paul always relished new challenges. By this point he'd been recognised as one of the top hotel managers in the world, and his skills were in high demand. In the late 1990s, he added two resorts to his already acclaimed CV, managing the Mount Buller Ski Resort and prestigious Day Dream Island in the Whitsundays.

Despite his immense success in Australia, Paul was always there for our family. Mum died in 1999 after a GP's misdiagnosis whilst Paul was enjoying a well-earned trip back home, and to my surprise he decided to stay for the next year, putting his career to one side in order to care for my father and help me run the Garden Lodge. This speaks volumes about the selfless man that Paul truly was.

Beyond this, my brother was incredibly humble and always happy to turn his talents to any job – regardless of whether it was seemingly beneath him. During that impromptu year in the UK, he gave up prestigious international hotel management to cook fish and chips on the seafront and even worked as a chef at a local nursing home. I'll never forget how nervous he was at the prospect of baking cakes for the elderly residents.

"They want me to bake cakes, Susan," he said, "but I've never made a cake!"

"Well, you will just have to learn then won't you!" I responded.

Later Paul brought us a sample of the carrot cake he'd made and it turned out to be the best I'd ever tasted. Paul was immensely caring and wanted to do his best at whatever he turned his hand to. For a man who was used to managing hundreds of staff at world-renowned hotels, this says a lot about his character.

Once Dad found his feet again, Paul decided to gain some experience in Asia in order to cement his status as one of the top hotel managers in the world. In 2001 he relocated to Bali to manage two establishments, The Mabisa and The Saphir.

With my husband Ron on our first trip to Bali to visit Paul

Paul with Sir Tom Jones at The Hotel Como in Melbourne

***

Two days after the blast, Ririn – Paul's PA – phoned to confirm that she had found Paul's body at Sanglah Hospital in Denpasar. She'd spent the day unzipping dozens of body bags in a painstaking effort to locate my brother, and I can't express the gratitude I feel towards her for what she must've gone through.

Paul was walking his regular route between The Mabisa and The Saphir at the time of the attack. Upon finishing his shift, he'd always walk on foot in the cool Balinese evening to whichever hotel he hadn't been managing that day, always putting the wellbeing of his staff and customers before his own leisure time. It was a route that led directly past the Sari Club, where the car bomb was detonated at 11.05pm. Paul was killed instantly.

5

THE AFTERMATH

The days following Paul's death are a painful blur. I was grief-stricken, in a state of shock and in constant floods of tears for my poor brother. Despite this, I had no time to grieve. There were so many questions to answer amidst so much confusion.

Despite Paul's staff locating his body, the Foreign Office refused to fly him home until they had secured DNA samples and dental records. This saga unnecessarily prolonged our pain over the next three weeks, turning our heartache into a living nightmare. During that time they assigned us with a family liaison officer, whose purpose was to keep us updated and informed as the logistics unfolded. Of course, they were completely useless and inevitably came to rely on me for information. *It should've been the other way around.*

To make the situation worse, they expected us to contribute £6000 towards the cost of bringing Paul home and refused to fly my father back from Spain. In the end, my poor dad had to organise and pay for his own flights amidst the heartache of losing his only son, and I will never forgive Jack Straw and the Foreign Office for their neglect during those first few days.

The only politician who proved to be a light in the dark at this point was Michael Howard MP, who I'd contacted shortly after the bomb exploded. He was disgusted at the way the Foreign Office was handling the situation, and I will never forget the relief I felt when he organised for the government to bring Paul home. From then on, Michael was God and I remain indebted to him. In the years following Paul's death, I was a guest speaker for him many times, most notably at the Conservative Spring Forum at The Grand in Brighton, where I introduced him in front of the entire Conservative party.

***

Despite the fact that the Foreign Office had finally organised for Paul's body to be brought home, my brother's estranged wife had shown up in Bali and was repeatedly preventing the plane from taking off. My parents never liked her, and I imagine she had shown up in order to stake her claim to Paul's various properties in Australia. In the end, they had to fly his body out in the middle of the night. She joins a long list of people whom I will never forgive for adding to our suffering.

Thankfully, Paul was friends with a funeral director, and

she contacted me to say that she would have everything taken care of in time for Paul's arrival. Neither myself or my father saw his body when he arrived at the funeral parlour. Although Paul's PA had said that his face was intact aside from some blood around his mouth, other reports informed us that Paul was missing from the waist down. We were told not to look, and we will never know the truth.

Despite the brutal reality of Paul's murder, I still dream that one day he's going to turn up at the door. I still dream of him telling me that he'd just lost his memory and now he's finally come home.

***

It's easy to overlook the fact that the chaos, grief and anger I was experiencing during those first few weeks was caught in a national media storm. The Bali bombing was the biggest news story in the world, and I had the newspapers and TV cameras constantly on my doorstep, constantly asking questions. Although this added to the stress of the situation, added stress was the least of my concerns. I always took the time to speak to the media. In my view, it was important to share my experience and draw public attention to the ongoing mishandling of my brother's death. You can still find those articles on various news sites, including *The Times*, the *Independent* and the BBC. I think they valued the way I spoke my mind, and I stand by every word.

My relationship with the media has continued in the years since Paul's death. The *Sun* even took me to Bali in the wake of the second bombing in 2005. I'll never forget how disgusting the hospital was. The relatives of the victims had to help care for their injured loved ones and sleep in the hospital corridors. Of course, The *Sun* had paid for the trip, which meant they had exclusive access to me, but thankfully they allowed me to accept a dinner invitation from the British Ambassador, Charles Humphrey.

In many ways, I became one of the go-to interviewees among the families of the British victims of the bombings, and my contributions appeared on TV as well as in the newspapers. I gave interviews for *Tonight with Trevor McDonald*, Sky World and *Newsnight* with Jeremy Paxman. I did a big piece with Martin Bell at Meridian called *The Big Story* as well as segments for ITV. Beyond this, I have lost track of the number of times I have been interviewed for local news programmes over the years.

Although it was vital for me to draw attention to the gross shortcomings of the UK government, this is contrasted by an immense gratitude I feel towards the Australians. By the time Paul's body was home, I'd written to John Howard – the Australian Prime Minister – in Canberra. He called me directly and sincerely apologised that Paul had not been properly acknowledged as an Australian citizen. From that moment onwards, the Australians were fantastic. They paid for Paul's funeral and paid for me to have counselling when the British government refused to do so. Moreover, they have contributed substantially towards our efforts to build a peace park on the site of the Sari Club. I am the current UK Ambassador for the Bali Peace Park project – something I hope my story will be able to help draw some much-needed support for.

***

Despite our ongoing torment, the nation began to grieve as the dust settled on the tragedy. Dad and I were invited by Prince Charles to Highgrove along with other victims' families, and whilst it was a strange experience to be drinking Pimm's and touring the Royal Gardens, I knew that it was a precious opportunity to speak to the man at the top. Prince Charles was a very diligent host, and we were informed that he wouldn't leave until he'd spoken to everyone who wanted an audience with him. I think most of the victims' family members were a little overwhelmed by the pomp and ceremony and could only bring themselves to express their gratitude for his hospitality. I thought otherwise: *I might only get one chance, I have to go for it*. My mum had always told me to go for the man at the top if you want to get anything done!

"Thank you for inviting us," I said, "but in truth, you're one of the only people who has shown us any compassion."

"What do you mean?" said Prince Charles, perhaps a little taken aback.

I seized the opportunity and explained the hardships we'd endured from the Foreign Office, which was met with genuine disbelief from the Prince. He directed me to write to his Private Secretary, Sir Michael Peat, who organized for the Red Cross to pay for us to visit Bali for the first memorial service.

Dad was also fond of Prince Charles. The first time we met him was at the memorial service at Southwark Cathedral, where they spoke at length about my dad's regiment. I think he liked my dad's no-nonsense attitude. Dad always wore his regimental tie with pride, which Prince Charles immediately recognized.

"Well you should do, Sir," replied Dad, "You are our Commander in Chief!"

As it happened, Prince Charles had spent the morning with the regiment, and from then on he'd always seek out my Dad at the various memorial services and events. We were his guests at Clarence House, and Dad was impressed at how Charles remembered who he was, who Paul was and the nature of their past conversations. Given that the Prince's schedule is an endless itinerary of royal engagements, this meant a lot to us. I think Charles will make an excellent king.

Of course, Dad's ability to speak his mind also came in handy with the public figures he disliked. I'll never forget the moment that Margaret Thatcher walked into St Paul's Cathedral for the Australian memorial service. We were sitting right behind Prince Philip and the Queen, and upon spotting the Iron Lady, Dad said (rather loudly), "What the bloody hell is she doing here?"

I was equally direct with the politicians who I've met over the years. The first time I met Jack Straw – then Foreign Secretary – was at the Southwark memorial service. I was introduced to him by Suzanne Hill, a member of the Foreign Office, who cautiously informed him how upset I was with the way the tragedy was being handled. Over the years I have felt repeatedly let down by Jack Straw. He told the United Kingdom Bali Bombings Victims Group (UKBBVG) that we would receive compensation from the Indonesian government, which made little sense to us. If UK nationals are killed in domestic terrorist attacks, the government compensates their families, and it was abhorrent that they refused to do the same for us just because our family members were killed abroad. Moreover, it's the responsibility of the Foreign Office to keep British nationals safe and informed across the world. We knew that they were well aware of the terrorist threat in Bali at the time of the bombings, yet MI6 neglected to raise the threat level. Meanwhile, both the USA and Australia had issued travel warnings for visitors to the island, and I often wonder if my brother would still be alive had the UK done the same. Needless to say, when I met Jack Straw for the first time, I told him that I could've punched him. There was no love lost between us.

Eventually, upon being advised by my lawyers in

Australia that we should seek legal representation, the law firm Allen and Overy took on the United Kingdom Bali Bombings Victims Group on a pro bono basis. We wanted compensation for the 33 British lives unnecessarily lost. We wanted a public enquiry into the failings of the Foreign Office, followed by a public apology. We wanted a memorial in the UK and funding towards the proposed Peace Park on the site of the bombing. We wanted mental health support and grief counseling.

Despite the fact that they took on our case, it often felt like Allen and Overy were on the government's side. Our meetings seemed to go round in circles without ever really getting anywhere. It was incredibly frustrating to spend those long, heart-wrenching hours caught in a legal loop with no end in sight. I have often felt in the years since that the law firm may have been under the thumb of the government in an attempt to subdue our voices. I remember leaving one particularly horrible meeting and feeling completely broken. I just sat on the stairs inside Waterstones at Charing Cross and cried my eyes out.

We have never received compensation for what happened and justice has always fallen short. In 2005, Abu Bakar Bashir – the so-called spiritual mastermind behind the group who coordinated the attack – was jailed for a mere 30 months. That amounts to four days in prison for each person killed. Meanwhile, the leader of Jemiah Islamiyah – the terrorist organization responsible for the bombing –

remains in custody at Guantanamo Bay. Although three of the perpetrators were executed by firing squad, others had their sentences overturned in botched constitutional hearings.

The survivors group has thankfully been able to contribute towards some positive change. The Foreign Office invited us to help them review their procedures in order to ensure that what we went through never happens again, and in 2006 a memorial was unveiled in London to commemorate the 202 victims of the attack.

Nowadays the group rarely meets. The battle we've endured over the past two decades has left us feeling tired and defeated, and you can't keep struggling against the tide forever. In many ways, I could fill an entire book with our pursuit for justice and my experiences with various officials over the years. The reality however is that this part of the story will never feel complete, and there is no happy ending to write.

The Official Residences of The Queen
Buckingham Palace Windsor Castle

The Official Residence of The Prince of Wale:
Clarence House

CLARENCE HOUSE

Please present this ticket at the visitors' entrance to Clarence House

on **MONDAY 02-AUG-2004**
at **11:45**

Guest of The Prince of Wales

Booking Reference: 1284901
Not for resale   VAT No. GB 597 4495 73

See reverse for Terms and Conditions

His Royal Highness The Prince ef *Wales requests the pleasure* ef *the company* ef

........CMr.Jo.5.epfuXu.>J..flj.*tr. .r-*...........

*at a Reception
to be held at The Orchard Room, Highgrove
on Friday, 25th July 2003*

R.S.V.P.
Please use return *card enclosed*

Time:3.30 pm
Dress: Lounge Suit

Myself with Camilla, Duchess of Cornwall, my husband, my daughter Stephanie and her husband at the National Memorial Arboretum

Susan and Dad at Highgrove with HRH Prince Charles

HOME COMFORTS: Sue Cooper and her family are delighted with their big success in the South East England tourism awards

The Garden Lodge

One of our famous guests, Brian Bovell. He starred in 'Gimme Gimme Gimme!'

6

LOOKING FORWARD

Ron and I remained close in the years which followed the tragedy, but I know that he struggled in his own way. I spent so much time and effort in the pursuit of justice that he had to take a more hands-on role in running the guesthouse, which he found particularly difficult. Opening the Garden Lodge was my dream, not his, and I know he didn't share my love of the business.

Ron's quiet frustration with my preoccupation also boiled down to the fact that he'd never really liked Paul. I think in many ways he was intimidated by my brother's success, guarding himself against this by keeping an emotional distance from Paul when he was alive. It must've been hard for Ron that my brother's death became my primary focus in the years which followed. Despite this, he remained supportive of me and rarely complained about the situation regardless of how he felt inside, and we persevered as a team.

Stephanie was deeply impacted by Paul's murder. She

was in her first year of college at the time and had dreams of becoming an accountant, but the way in which the tragedy hijacked our family greatly took its toll on her. She began to suffer with anxiety and was unable to reconcile the ongoing trauma in time to focus on her studies. Having spent the last three months of 2002 dealing with the mess of the tragedy, the prospect of returning in the new year became increasingly daunting for her. This was made all the worse by the fact that her teachers gave her highly critical and insensitive reviews in her end-of-term reports. Despite the fact that I'd informed the college office of what was going on, the message had never been passed on to her teachers. Of course, this infuriated me, and I contacted the late Tessa Jowell who'd previously served as the Minister of State for the Department for Education and Skills. Although she sorted everything out –no questions asked – the ordeal was all too much for Stephanie, and she never returned to college. It deeply saddened me that my brother's murder ruined my daughter's education.

Despite this, Stephanie was an incredible support for me in the years following Paul's death. I was amazed at the way she willingly accompanied me to various legal meetings and memorial events, which would've been an intimidating prospect for any teenager. She sang 'Wind Beneath my Wings' at the cleansing ceremony in Kuta on the first anniversary of the bombing, bringing victims' families and politicians alike to tears. Moreover, Stephanie was an immense help to me in running the business, and I feel an incredible gratitude for everything she did in the wake of Paul's death.

***

Despite everything that was going on, the Garden Lodge remained a functioning family business in the years following the tragedy. It helped to keep me grounded at home and gave a vital sense of purpose to my heartbroken father. Despite the fact that he was in his 80s, he still did everything he could to help me and took great pride in building a brick barbecue in our garden. At heart, Dad was still a bricklayer.

In 2009 however, the reputation of the guesthouse – as well as my own – was called into question when we were featured on an episode of *The Hotel Inspector*. I received a call from Channel 5 asking if we'd like to be featured, and while this initially appeared to be an exciting prospect, Alex Polizzi – the so-called 'inspector' – turned out to be a real piece of work. The programme was framed as though we'd contacted the show because we were a 'failing business', and she was very critical of our style and setup.

I later learned that the show had contacted us because the producers had seen my numerous interview pieces in the wake of the bombing. They knew I would speak my mind and make for good TV, which in hindsight all feels rather dishonest. Whilst I can certainly admit to owning a lot of ornaments and being truthful to a fault, the Garden

Lodge was portrayed as a clutter-filled establishment under the rule of a stubborn hoarder. It was very painful for us when the programme aired, and I have received dozens of abusive comments, messages and phone calls over the years because of how I was characterized. I hated the way our business was treated like a joke.

Over the years however, it became increasingly difficult for us to compete with the rise of bland budget hotels, and my life was once again turned upside down when I suffered a severe stroke in 2010.

I didn't fully understand what was happening to me at the time. It was a morning like any other, and I was in the bathroom getting ready prior to our usual breakfast service when the stroke happened. I was rushed to hospital with Oliver driving in pursuit of the ambulance. Ron was in bits but had to stay behind to cook breakfast. We'd learnt the hard way over the years that the public didn't really care about us in moments of hardship. Years prior, I'd attempted to cancel dinner service after receiving the call to say that my mum was dying in hospital. There were plenty of restaurants nearby, yet the guests had no sympathy and expected me to stay and cook for them.

The stroke was very severe and the doctors were surprised that I survived. I spent the next six months in hospital, gradually regaining my ability to walk. Despite this, the stroke has left me permanently disabled. I have never regained use of my left side, and my mobility is severely restricted. Moreover, the stroke has impacted my memory – something which is unbelievably frustrating for someone who has always relied on their sharp recall.

Ultimately, I know that the stroke was caused by the stress and heartache of Paul's murder. I was only 58 and relatively healthy. This is exactly what I mean when I say that the victims' families all received life sentences.

Over the past decade it's been incredibly hard to come to terms with my disability. Basic tasks are an immense challenge, and I long for the days when I could take charge of a kitchen, travel with ease and take complete care of myself. Health is something you can never take for granted.

***

Ron died on 9th August 2011. He'd gone into St James' Hospital after a routine appointment where it was discovered that he needed a replacement aorta valve. According to the doctors he probably wouldn't make it through the operation but would certainly die without it. Ron survived the operation but caught an infection in the theatre. He deteriorated quickly but kept hanging on, even when given his last rights.

Whilst losing Ron was difficult, I was suffering so much in the wake of my stroke that it was hard to truly process his death. I had suffered so much, and the pain all seemed to blur together.

Although we remained closer than ever, Dad was never the same following Paul's death. My brother became his sole topic of conversation, and my stroke hit him particularly hard. I'd always been the apple of his eye, and it must've been incredibly hard to see his surviving child suffer so much. Dad passed away in 2014, and in many ways I think he died of a broken heart.

Eventually I decided to permanently close the Garden Lodge in 2017. Although I took on staff in the wake of my stroke, the business inevitably struggled and became too much for me to manage.

***

It might seem that my life has almost entirely consisted of hardship since Paul's death, yet there have been many precious moments and memories amidst the pain, precious moments which have always proven to be a light in the dark. I strongly believe that we must play the cards we are dealt, and I will always try to make the best of a bad hand.

All in all I have visited Bali 13 times since the bombing. People might wonder why I try to visit the island where my brother died each year, and I certainly shared their concerns on that first trip with my father in 2003. It was immensely scary to consider how I might feel about being so close to the site of his murder, yet the reality has always been the polar opposite of my fears. Bali is where I feel closest to Paul. It is a beautiful place where he was known and loved. When I visit the hotels which he managed, I feel as though I am walking in his footsteps. When I connect with those who knew him, I feel connected to him.

I remember the cleansing ceremony in Kuta on the one-year anniversary of the bombings, a painfully hot day where the bombsite was decorated with religious ornaments and a ritual slaughter of water buffalo and chickens took place on the beach. Despite these unusual traditions, it was a very special occasion and a wonderful group-gesture from the Balinese people. There was a beautiful service in the multi-denominational church on the hill, with all the fantastic Australian politicians in attendance. They paid for various aspects of the memorial, including golden garudas and a memorial pond. There I met Baroness Crawley – the government's representative – a friendly woman despite her status who simply said, "Call me Christine."

John Howard – the former Australian Prime Minister – was also in attendance with his wife. I didn't want to approach him because I was in floods of tears, but as it happened he was crying more than me! I've always been touched by the way he shared the victims' families' emotions of the tragedy.

The Australians were incredibly wonderful and chartered a plane to fly us to their own memorial in Canberra. We all lit a candle and placed them at the front of the service, and by the end there were so many that they set the curtains ablaze! Thankfully it was a minor fire, and we all shared a laugh as panicked staff swarmed the curtain, fire extinguishers in hand.

Later we were all taken by coach to the Governor General's residence to meet the other Australian families, with absolutely no media present. Paul's fellow hoteliers provided us with accommodation and a free car hire, as well as a complimentary stay in Sydney. It's a big contrast to the Brits, who did sod all!

This generosity from the Australians runs from politicians to business leaders and even distant family members. After the bombing I called my cousin Carolyn in Australia who I'd never met. She was a nanny to a lawyer's children, and her employer agreed to take on our case for free in order to get Paul's Australian estate settled. Carolyn and I have remained incredibly close since the bombing, although Paul's estranged wife made it incredibly difficult for us to get things sorted.

All in all, I have countless magical memories of Bali. On one of our trips to Bali for a memorial service, we released hundreds of baby turtles into the sea with the man who was the Chief of Police at the time of the bombing. He later went on to become the Governor of Bali. Later, in 2012 the Australian government paid for all Australian families to go to Bali for the tenth anniversary memorial services. They also paid for Val to go as my supporter, and we received armed protection as well as sole use of the only wheelchair-accessible taxi in the country. We stayed at the beautiful

Discovery Kartika Plaza Hotel, which has since become our home in Bali. On that occasion, we met Julia Gillard – another wonderful Australian Prime Minister – and Marty Natalegawa.

Of course, there were a few Brits I liked too. Jim Lidell – Her Majesty's Consul General – was waiting to speak to me when I landed in Bali following the bombing, but I had little patience for British politicians and ordered him to wait his turn! Despite this, we became great friends and we still joke about that infamous first meeting. He even organised an 18th birthday cake for Stephanie when she celebrated her birthday in Bali.

That said, my interactions with numerous political figures are only one side of the story, and there are dozens of wonderful people whom I have got to know through the tragedy. Russell Ward is someone I still greatly admire. He was a fireman on holiday at the time of the bombing and stopped the diggers going in to clear the rubble in the knowledge that survivors might be buried amidst it. He later helped to lead the survivors' group and was later awarded an MBE as well as a Pride of Britain award for his efforts. Of course, Russell was supported by other wonderful people like Stuart Strong, a New Zealander who aided him in the wake of the tragedy.

For all our shared pain and frustration, that same survivors' group has gifted me other wonderful friends like Sandra and Bob Empson, with whom I have shared an incredible connection since the tragedy. Then there are Paul's fantastic staff, whose stories are too numerous to mention yet incredibly precious for me. From the girls he trained, who often tell me stories of Paul's kindness, generosity and calmness, to his PA, Ririn, who we later took on holiday to Australia. Then there was Ed, Paul's best friend in Australia who tracked me down via the Samaritans and Michael Howard. I was touched when Ed flew to the anniversary in Canberra in order to meet me, bringing with him David Perry – my brother's protégé. Paul must've done a good job, because David now manages the prestigious Windsor Hotel in Melbourne, where we were provided with a complimentary champagne high tea during one of our many visits.

There are so many names and stories of the people who knew Paul I could mention here. From the Balinese protestors who marched on the prison in his name, to the publisher Elizabeth Siboro, who confessed to loving my brother and still calls me sister, as well as Roy at the Bush Telegraph where Paul used to drink. Despite this however, my story must move forward.

***

I was blessed to find love again when I met my second husband, Richard, through the internet on MatchAffinity. com in 2015. I like to think that Paul would be proud of this given my track record with technology! I was very sceptical of course, particularly given the fact that Richard was 60 miles away in Tunbridge Wells – I'd specified that I only wanted someone within a 30-mile radius!

As you might expect, I was brutally honest about myself on my profile, but Richard was keen for us to meet regardless. He visited me shortly after, and following a quick once-over from a friend and a carer, we had a lunch date followed by a grand tour of Folkestone. Afterwards, we sat in the lounge talking for god knows how long. I certainly liked him, but I couldn't get rid of him – I had to phone my carer from another room to come and get me ready for bed, just so he would leave!

From then on Richard visited me every Thursday. Of course, the first time I visited him and his family I was petrified – just as I had been at the prospect of meeting Ron's family all those years earlier. Thankfully my mind was put at ease when his sister toasted us over champagne at lunch. "Welcome to the family!" she said.

Richard and I were married in Bali on 14th November 2015, in a beautiful ceremony organised by the then retired Her Majesty's Consular General Jim Liddell – the same man I'd told to 'wait his turn' all those years earlier. Thankfully, Richard loves to travel as much as me, and before our wedding we visited his brother in Brisbane; Carolyn in Sydney; and his son Sam in Melbourne, where we had to stay longer than planned because of a volcanic eruption preventing flights to Bali. Fortunately, we were also able to visit my dear friend Betty Radstake, as well as Paul's best friend, Ed, who took us to Hotel Como. There, we toasted Paul in the Champagne Bar, and Ed told us many stories about Paul. He could never forget the time Paul invited him for breakfast at the Como. Ed was busy but Paul insisted, and when he arrived there were press and photographers everywhere. Ed joked that he didn't realise he was that famous, and after fighting his way into Paul's office, he found my brother having breakfast with the man whom all the fuss was about – Jackie Chan!

I'll never forget our wonderful trip around Europe, where we stayed consecutively with Daniel & Genevieve; Olivia; John & Monique; and Delphine. It was wonderful to visit so many of the precious friends I'd made over the years, and I remain grateful to have them in my life. Through Richard I have also gained two wonderful stepchildren in Jessica and Sam, and five step-grandchildren in Sienna, Jamie, Amelia, Joshua and Harry.

I am immensely proud of my own children too. Stephanie has gone on to forge a successful career in the hospitality industry and currently manages a pub in Sudbury, Suffolk and is currently national gaming manager at Stonegate group. Oliver lives with me in Folkestone and has just finished writing his 28th book!

***

I have lost a lot in life, and the pain of my brother's murder never really goes away. The reality is that I may never find the justice I seek, I may never fully recover from my stroke and I will never be able to leave the Garden Lodge as a successful, flourishing business for my children. Despite this, I have found that there are always lights in the dark, however black things may seem. From my wonderful friends, to my beautiful children. From my beloved memories as a chef and business owner, to the precious moments which have connected me to my wonderful brother. To those who have given light to my story, I thank each of you from the bottom of my heart.

Paul, my soul will always hurt for you, and I will always lament the fact that you were taken from us far too soon. Despite this, I will never forget you, and I will never forget the joy that you brought to this world. I know that your life was cut short, but I know that it was a life well-lived. I hope my words in this book are a fitting tribute to you, wherever you are.

Paul

Story Terrace

Made in United States
Orlando, FL
19 October 2024